THE MISSIONAL PASTOR'S HANDBOOK

Tim Jackson

New Harbor Press
Rapid City, SD

Copyright © 2025 Tim Jackson

All rights reserved. No part of this publication may be reproduced, distributed or transmitted in any form or by any means, including photocopying, recording, or other electronic or mechanical methods, without the prior written permission of the publisher, except in the case of brief quotations embodied in critical reviews and certain other non-commercial uses permitted by copyright law. For permission requests, write to the publisher, addressed "Attention: Permissions Coordinator," at the address below.

New Harbor Press
1601 Mt Rushmore Rd, Ste 3288
Rapid City, SD 57701
www.newharborpress.com

Ordering Information:
Quantity sales. Special discounts are available on quantity purchases by corporations, associations, and others. For details, contact the "Special Sales Department" at the address above.

The Missional Pastor's Handbook/Jackson —1st ed.

ISBN 978-1-63357-473-1

First edition: 10 9 8 7 6 5 4 3 2 1

Unless otherwise noted, all Scripture quotations are taken from the Christian Standard Bible®, Copyright © 2017 by Holman Bible Publishers. Used by permission. Christian Standard Bible®, and CSB® are federally registered trademarks of Holman Bible Publishers.

Contents

What is a Missional Pastor? 1

Surrender 7

Service 13

Sowing 19

Sacraments 25

Sent 33

Sincere 41

Sheep 47

Skilled Master Builder 55

Steadfast 63

The Samaritan's Purse 69

Epilogue: 77

Prologue

What is a Missional Pastor?

With captivating stories, timeless biblical principles, and actionable steps, this handbook promises to transform local pastors into inspiring missional leaders within their hearts, homes, churches, and communities. Experience a journey of transformation that equips you to fulfill your divine purpose in every aspect of pastoral life.

> All Scripture is inspired by God and is profitable for teaching, for rebuking, for correcting, for training in righteousness, so that the man of God may be complete, equipped for every good work. (2 Timothy 3:16–17)

First, let's set out some clear definitions for what it means to be missional and what it means to be a pastor.

Missional: A Christian term that describes a missionary lifestyle. Being missional includes embracing the posture, thinking, behaviors, and practices of a missionary to reach others with the gospel.

Essentially, the idea of being missional teaches that the church has a mission because Jesus had a mission.

What was Jesus' mission?

For the Son of Man has come to seek and to save the lost. (Luke 19:10)

Pastor: The word *pastor* comes from a Latin word which means "shepherd." In Ephesians 4:11, Paul identifies shepherding "pastors" as one function in the church along with teaching, missionary work, evangelism, and prophecy.

As I walked along the familiar streets of our new neighborhood in East Knoxville, each step carried with it a prayer, an intention to deeply connect with the lives of those around me. The sidewalks were uneven, the houses worn, but homes nonetheless, filled with the stories and struggles of those who lived there. Pausing to greet a neighbor, I felt the mission in my heart, one that Jesus Himself had lived: to seek and save those who are lost, to make His love known where it felt distant.

This is what I believe a missional pastor must be—a shepherd who embraces the role of a missionary, living out this mission in every aspect of their day, be it at home, at work, or even during play.

In 2006, I was serving as an associate pastor to a thriving local church while my wife was working as a nurse. We felt called to leave our highly successful careers to plant a missional church.

We purchased an old, rundown home in an urban community, enrolled our kids in the local schools, and formed an agreement with a local skate park to host our worship services on Sundays and our youth outreach on Wednesdays.

Our friends and family thought we had lost our minds. We had, in a way, traded the American Dream for the mission of Christ.

I had noticed over the last ten years that new churches were being planted, but it seemed they were always in white-collar neighborhoods.

No one was planting churches in areas where people were living on the margins and desperate for the gospel of Jesus Christ.

I remember growing up in areas like the ones we moved into, poor neighborhoods that seemed to have no hope. No one knocked on our doors and invited my family to church in those neighborhoods. This challenged community was where we felt God calling us to plant our lives and family. And that is what we did.

Shortly after moving into the neighborhood, I began to prayer walk in our community to meet our socially diverse neighbors and to make new friends.

After a few months, we bought a grill for less than fifty dollars, bought hamburgers and hot dogs, and walked through the neighborhood to invite our new neighbors to a cookout at our home.

Nearly everyone showed up at our house that August evening at 6 p.m. Many of them brought drinks, chips, and other items that went well with our grilled food.

Before the meal, I told my neighbors we had been praying for them, praying for our neighborhood, and that I was a pastor who was starting a church for people just like us. We prayed over the meal and spent the next three hours getting to know one another. In total, twenty-five of our new neighbors showed up for that first cookout.

Over the next four years, we invested in our neighbors, our neighborhood, and our community. Every two or three months, we would host a cookout or an indoor dinner, depending on the weather. Our front yard and our small home were often filled with our neighbors, who had quickly become our friends.

During that time, we built strong relationships. We prayed with our neighbors, led them to faith, baptized them, and saw them join our small, local neighborhood church.

Four years after we moved out of the neighborhood and to another state, one of our neighbors called us to tell my wife and me that the neighborhood was still gathering for cookouts, fellowship, and prayer.

There were churches all around our neighborhood in our small city, but I didn't see them engaging in their community to build relationships to share the gospel. In short, I didn't see missional pastors or missional living from the churches that were in our community. According to a recent survey, only 25% of churches in urban areas implement community outreach programs, highlighting a noticeable gap in engagement and active ministry within local neighborhoods. Imagine walking through the streets surrounding your church and observing the lives unfolding there, untouched by the light of loving ministry. What street within a mile of your building remains untouched, a reminder of missed opportunities to extend the gospel? This lack of involvement means that many opportunities to connect with and serve the surrounding community remain untapped. Confronted with this stark reality, it becomes imperative for us to awaken a sense of urgency and commitment towards living out our missional calling.

At many conferences I attended during those years, I only occasionally heard speakers discuss the missional engagement of the neighborhoods around their churches. Most speakers focused on growth, but not on missional growth, the way Jesus and the Ancient Church intended, as we find in the Book of Acts.

So, over the last twenty-five years, I have refined a missional focus and mindset that has served me well in the small towns and large cities that I have been honored to serve in. I have tweaked it from time to time depending on the needs of the local communities and cultures.

I sat down to write this small book to place in the hands of local pastors who are looking for a rhythm of life and ministry that honors God, their calling, and the church, as well as the neighborhoods and communities where He has placed them.

It is my sincere belief that if one applies themselves to the principles found within, they will live a life and lead a ministry that bears much fruit.

In Romans 14:12, Paul tells the church that each of us will give an account of ourselves to God. As a Christian and as a pastor, I want to give a good account of the time, energy, and resources our Heavenly Father has graciously given me.

I want to live a life that bears so much fruit that it brings glory to God and proves to the world around me that I am a disciple of Jesus Christ. (John 15:8)

So, take your time reading through each step in this process, a process that you can apply to yourself each week. It's an iterative process, one that will transform you steadily into the image of Christ for the glory of God and for the gracious benefit of those around you.

CHAPTER 1

Surrender

Eric Liddlell, a life surrendered for the glory of God

In the 1924 Olympics in Paris, France, the favorite to win the 100-meter race, Scotsman Eric Liddell, refused to compete due to the competition being held on the Sabbath. Instead, he ran in the 400-meter race later that week and won the gold medal.

One of his most famous quotes was, "God made me fast. And when I run, I feel His pleasure."

After the Olympics, Eric returned to China with his family, where he served as a Christian missionary until he died in 1945.

Surrender: An action which involves ceasing resistance, giving up, or abandoning oneself to someone or something else.

I did not grow up in a local church. My family had been broken and scattered by trauma. These unfortunate events sent my mom drifting across the southeast, and we were right there with her.

We were constantly moving from city to city, from town to town, from neighborhood to neighborhood. I attended around fifteen different schools from the first grade to the ninth grade, some of them more than once. I failed the fourth grade in large part due to being homeless.

On my final night in my home, my mom's husband, under the heavy influence of alcohol, beat her severely. She was hospitalized, but she did not press charges.

This cycle of abuse had been going on for years, and I was often involved in their arguments in one way or another. I had had enough.

So, I left. I didn't run away from home; I just left. I was only sixteen. I forged my birth certificate, got a new driver's license that stated I was eighteen (there were no computers at the DMV in the 1980s), got two jobs, and rented an apartment.

What does a young man do with no boundaries, his own money, and his own apartment? He does whatever he wants to. And I did. I made a lot of mistakes and hurt a lot of people.

Within a few years, I realized I needed an education. So, I enlisted in the Army, got my GED, and began to attend college. After leaving the Army, I was pursuing my bachelor's degree in Chattanooga, Tennessee, when I met a brilliant young woman. We were married less than a year later.

I believed I had "cleaned up" my life. So, when we were invited to church a few years later while at a friend's wedding, we declined. However, our two daughters really wanted to go. So, reluctantly, we made our way to church that Sunday morning in August of 1996.

Smiling, happy people met us at the door. There were people there to take our kids and sign them in as well. When we sat down, those sitting nearby greeted us warmly. The music moved us, and the message seemed to be speaking directly to us as we drove to church that morning. God was present in that place, and my wife and I knew it.

So, we came back that evening and again that Wednesday. We were hooked. Two months later, on a Tuesday night in October, during a revival at the church, I surrendered my life to Jesus Christ as my Lord and Savior. I confessed my sins, and asked and received His forgiveness, love, and grace.

My willingness to surrender my life and to accept Jesus' abundant and eternal life has changed my life forever.

Eighteen months later, on a rainy Saturday night in Knoxville, Tennessee, at a Promise Keepers rally, I sensed God's call on my life into pastoral ministry. God affirmed that call the next day in our church service. I came forward at the end of the service and surrendered myself to His call on my life as a local pastor and shepherd. Both the call to follow Christ and the call to be a pastor have shaped who I am and how I live every day.

I would like to say my surrender was welcomed with open arms. It was not. My wife struggled with that call to ministry for the next six years, until one night God spoke to her and she, in turn, woke me up and told me she was ready to stand beside me as I embraced my calling.

From 1997 to 2002, I worked part-time in ministry. I had avoided full-time opportunities due to my wife's pushback on my calling. But within a couple of days of her acceptance of the call and her stating her willingness to stand beside me, I was offered a full-time job at a wonderful local church. She had surrendered as well. God affirmed that calling and now she brings the heart of gospel with her each day to her medical practice.

When I made the transition into full-time ministry, I committed that my early morning hours would be a time of surrender to Christ and His plan and purpose for my life. My job had me up at 4 a.m. each morning, so I made that my surrender time.

> **Therefore, brothers and sisters, in view of the mercies of God, I urge you to present your bodies as a living sacrifice, holy and pleasing to God; this is your true worship. Do not be conformed to this age, but be transformed by the renewing of your mind, so that you may discern what is the good, pleasing, and perfect will of God. (Romans 12:1–2)**

Main Points of the Passage:

1. Paul pointed out to the church that God had poured out His mercies (plural) over them.
2. Paul argued that the reasonable response of the church, individually and collectively, was to offer our lives back to God as living sacrifices. This was our true act of worship.
3. Christ-followers were not to be like the world, but to be holy, and we come to holiness through the renewal of ourselves in the Word of God.

Only through this process of surrender and renewal would we understand the will of God.

Since early 2003, I have been waking up each morning, Sunday through Friday, at around 4 a.m. I brew some strong black coffee and find a place in my living room to kneel and recite Romans 12:1–2.

This daily surrender has profoundly impacted various aspects of my ministry. For instance, my early morning routine has sharpened my preaching, allowing me to connect more authentically with my congregation. With a clear mind and heart, I find my counseling sessions more insightful, addressing the needs of those in my care with deeper empathy. Moreover, daily commitment to this practice enhances my decision-making, guiding me to align my choices with our shared mission. The early mornings are not just a ritual but a powerful catalyst for tangible ministry fruit, evidenced by the growing engagement and transformation within our community. Surrendering my life, marriage, family, and pastoral ministry back to Christ every day has kept me fresh, focused, and faithful. Without that daily time of surrender, I am sure I would not remain so.

> Test yourselves to see if you are in the faith. Examine yourselves. Or do you yourselves not rec-

ognize that Jesus Christ is in you?—unless you fail the test. (2 Corinthians 13:5)

Questions for Reflection:

1. Have you surrendered your life to Jesus Christ and accepted Him as your Savior and Lord? If so, is that surrender to Jesus a distant memory or a present reality? Why not stop and thank Him right now for His gift of grace and surrender to Him once again?
2. Have you been called by Jesus into pastoral ministry? If so, have you surrendered your life to pastoral ministry? Is that surrender a distant memory or a present reality? Why not stop right now and thank Jesus for His call on your life into pastoral ministry and surrender it to Him?
3. Are you setting aside a daily time of surrender where you can meet with Jesus in prayer, study of His word, and reflect on your life and ministry? If not, why not plan on when you will begin to do so? This needs to be a place of silence, solitude, and free from distractions.
4. Are there earthly pursuits in your life that hinder or compromise your surrender to Jesus Christ as a Christian and as a pastor? If so, why not invite close friends into your life to hold you accountable for removing those pursuits?
5. Do you take the time to recognize all the goodness and mercy our Heavenly Father has poured into your life and give Him thanks and praise? If not, take the time now to do so.

Examining our lives as Christians and pastors keeps us fresh, focused, faithful, and fully surrendered.

A fully surrendered pastor is one who will embody his missional purpose where he lives, works, and plays, because God is actively at work within him and he is actively present with God.

Practical Steps for Application:

1. Create a surrender space in your daily life where you meet with God to surrender your life and ministry back to Him.
2. Examine your daily life, marriage, family, and pastoral ministry.
3. Give thanks and praise to God for all the good He has placed in your life. Try reading two or three Psalms each day to create a heart and mind of gratitude and praise.
4. Read a chapter of Proverbs each day to create a mind of knowledge, understanding, and wisdom.
5. Keep the person and work of the Trinity in front of you and pray to be holy as They are holy. Matthew 5–7 is foundational to being a Christ-follower for me.
6. Immerse yourself in the Word of God that you are teaching and preaching every day—not for your sermon's sake, but for your surrender and transformation.
7. Read books that are readily applicable to who Christ has called you to be. For me: Christ-follower, husband, father, pastor.

Final Thought:

Pastors who have surrendered to the call and mission of Christ will create marriages, families, and local churches that are surrendered as well.

CHAPTER 2

Service

A missional pastor is committed to loving and serving those our Heavenly Father has placed in their care.

For even the Son of Man did not come to be served, but to serve, and to give his life as a ransom for many. (Mark 10:45)

Missional Pastor Summation So Far:

Missional pastors live a life surrendered to the call of Jesus Christ; and, they love and serve those Jesus has placed in their care.

Where does the work of the missional pastor begin each day? I believe it starts in our home.

As an associate pastor at a thriving rural Southern Baptist Church in the early 2000s, I was given grace by our Heavenly Father and the local school system to start having lunch with students from our church.

This initiative was an immediate success, as I not only built strong relationships with our middle school and high school students but also established connections with their peers, school leadership, and teachers.

Within a few weeks, I was praying with the principals and teachers of the schools as well as the parents. Not long after that, I sat down with school leadership and was able to put into place our first campus ministries under the 1984 Equal Access Act.

Our ministries were sponsored by teachers who could not pray or lead Bible studies, but acted as hosts for the campus club we called Youth for Christ. They were led by students in prayer, song, and Bible study. Our church was joyful in its support—we even brought donuts!

Our Youth for Christ (YFC) at Norris Middle School exploded in growth. We soon had about fifteen students serving on the YFC leadership team and about one hundred to one hundred and fifty kids attending each week. We had a similar club at the high school that did very well, too.

It didn't take long for the word to spread about YFC in our school system. Other teachers, students, and parents wanted YFC in their schools. So, we began to plant Youth for Christ in different middle and high schools across the county. Then we were approached by elementary schools as well!

For the elementary school, we changed the club's name to Kids for Christ (KFC). We met with third-, fourth-, and fifth-grade students who wanted to be leaders on Mondays after school and trained them to lead.

KFC exploded across the county just like YFC, with some of their clubs achieving the highest number of weekly attendees. Parents of KFC students would sometimes meet in the parking lot to pray over their campuses while the kids were leading their peers.

Before long, I was asked to take the model of KFC and YFC to other campuses outside of our community. I recruited students from the local Bible college and from local churches around each campus where there was a desire to start a KFC or YFC program.

The next thing I knew, we were in multiple counties and two states. One of our high school's YFCs was averaging between one hundred and fifty to two hundred kids at their weekly club. This by far was our largest YFC club.

My own kids were leading a KFC and a YFC in their respective schools. It was an immensely proud moment for me as a father and as a missional pastor.

As these ministries grew and grew, I was spending less time focused on my marriage and my wife. Several (SEVERAL) times over a two-year period, she approached me about prioritizing our marriage. I kept telling her I would, but in truth I did not.

We stopped communicating; we argued more; our intimacy was nonexistent, like our prayer life. I do not know what the final straw was for my wife, but one morning after getting the kids off to school, she told me that she wanted a divorce. She no longer felt loved or cared for. She recognized that I had drifted far away from her, and she was no longer a priority for me. She promised a quiet divorce and told me I would not have to move out until it was completed.

We had been married sixteen years. We had five kids. We were debt-free. We were living in our dream home. I was leading the most influential campus ministry in East Tennessee, and my wife wanted a divorce. Why? Because I had stopped loving and serving her like Jesus loved and served the church.

In that moment, the Holy Spirit spoke to me and told me that if I let her walk out of my life, I would have lost the greatest gift He had placed in my hands to care for.

With a humble heart, I apologized. I asked for forgiveness and I promised my wife that if she didn't leave, she would be the priority of my love and service each and every day from that moment on.

In the quiet of that kitchen, she walked forward, and I did the same. I reached out and took her hands and prayed over our marriage. It took some time, but with a lot of love and hard work, within a year our marriage was stronger than ever. In that time, God called my wife into medical ministry as a doctor, and

I committed to making sure that she and our kids would be the priority moving forward as she made her way through medical school and residency.

Today, I am a missional pastor. My wife is a missional physician bringing the love of Christ to her medical team and patients each day. In that moment in our kitchen many years ago, Jesus reminded me what He taught His disciples on His final night on Earth.

> Before the Passover Festival, Jesus knew that his hour had come to depart from this world to the Father. Having loved his own who were in the world, he loved them to the end. So He got up from supper, laid aside his outer clothing, took a towel, and tied it around himself. Next, he poured water into a basin and began to wash his disciples' feet and to dry them with the towel tied around him. When Jesus had washed their feet and put on his outer clothing, he reclined again and said to them, "Do you know what I have done for you? You call me Teacher and Lord—and you are speaking rightly, since that is what I am. So if I, your Lord and Teacher, have washed your feet, you also ought to wash one another's feet. For I have given you an example that you also should do just as I have done for you. Truly I tell you. A servant is not greater than his master, and a messenger is not greater than the one who sent him. If you know these things, you are blessed if you do them." (John 13:1, 4–5, 12–17)

As missional pastors, we must simply follow the example of Jesus we find powerfully presented here in John: 13. He promises in verse 17 that we will be blessed if we do so.

Main Points of the Passage:
1. Jesus knew that He had come from God and was going back to God. You and I will give an account to God for the life and ministry He has placed in our hands (John 13:3, Romans 14:12). We need to keep this in front of ourselves each and every day.
2. Jesus loved His own with His all (John 13:1). Who are we called to love with our all? Those in our home, those in our church, and those in our community, especially the less fortunate (Matthew 25:31–40).
3. Jesus removed anything that might get in the way of His loving service to those in His care (John 13:4). Are there things in your life getting in the way of your loving service to your family, your church, or your community? Get rid of it.
4. Jesus humbled Himself to love and serve His own with His all. It takes humility to love and serve like Jesus.
5. Jesus instructed His disciples to follow His example and promised to bless them if they did. Is your life a reflection of Jesus' love and service to those in your care? Where do you sense He is blessing you as you do so?

Missional pastors need to remember that their missional service begins with their own home, their neighborhood, their local church, and the less fortunate in their own community.

A life that is congruent in love and service in each of these areas will be a powerful and present witness for Christ and His local church.

Questions for Reflection:
1. If today was your last day on Earth, would you be ready to give a good account of loving and serving those placed in your care? Why or why not?
2. Do the people in your care feel loved and served by you? Why or why not?
3. What things in your own life do you need to remove so you can love and serve those in your care better?
4. What are the tangible things you are doing to love and serve those in your care?
5. Is your life a living reflection of loving and serving as Jesus loved and served? Why or why not?

Practical Steps for Application:
1. Know who God has placed in your hands to love and serve.
2. Know how to love and serve those God has placed in your care.
3. Take steps each week to love and serve those God has placed in your care,
4. Invite others to help you love and serve those placed in your care.
5. Rest in knowing Jesus is pleased with those disciples of His who follow His example. He will bless you!

Final Thought:
Some people will take advantage of your selfless love and service (John 13:2). Love and serve them anyway.

CHAPTER 3

Sowing

Missional pastors are called to sow the seeds of the gospel generously and graciously where they live, work, and play, so that people may come to know and accept Jesus Christ as their Lord and Savior.

> Now the one that provides seed for the sower and bread for food will also provide and multiply your seed and increase the harvest of your righteousness. You will be enriched in every way for all generosity, which produces thanksgiving to God through us. For the ministry of this service is not only supplying the needs of the saints but is also overflowing in many expressions of thanks to God. (2 Corinthians 9:10–12)

Missional Pastor Summation So Far:
Missional pastors live a life surrendered to the call of Jesus Christ; love and serve those Jesus has placed in their care; and, sow with generosity and grace the Word of God over those in their care.

After my wife accepted God's call onto her life to become a missional physician, we picked up our little family and moved from Kentucky to Tennessee so that she could again attend medical school. While she was busy getting plugged into her first semester (which was around eighty-plus hours a week), I got our three kids enrolled in school, set up our home, and began to get to know the area.

I am a firm believer that God is always at work around you (a principle my wife and I learned from the book *Experiencing God* by Henry Blackaby). We don't do something and ask God to bless it, we look to see where God is at work and join Him in that good work.

So, I approached our local association office and began to meet with the director. I asked him where he saw God at work in their community, in their association, and in their own lives. I took notes.

In one of those meetings, I was invited by an area pastor to a local outreach meeting of other local pastors from a certain small town. It was going to be *ecumenical*, meaning there would be leaders from many different denominations.

It seemed that they had a thriving thrift-store ministry, and they met monthly to nail down details. So, I planned on attending. Again, I was looking to see where God was at work in my new community.

I showed up early and got to meet all the pastors from the town. As the meeting got underway, it was apparent that they were very proud of their thrift-store ministry. One church took leadership and management of the thrift store each week, and many underserved families and individuals benefited from the clothing, food, and furniture.

I was taking notes and realized about an hour into the meeting that in all the talk about the thrift store, no one had mentioned the gospel, prayer, or Jesus in connection with the ministry.

So, I did what I always did when we parachuted into a new town—I raised my hand to ask a question.

My first questions were, "What is the purpose of the thrift store? Does it have a purpose statement in connection with it?" There was no purpose statement, but they were all together in that the purpose of the thrift store was to help the underserved in their community, and it was doing just that.

I again raised my hand and asked if we offered to pray for those who came to the thrift store. One of the local churches in the area had a parking lot ministry that you could pay to park at for local events. They invited those who parked there for events to fill out a prayer request and put it in the money slot. Each week, that church got dozens of prayer requests from people. What a powerful ministry!

The question about prayer threw them for a loop. No, they did not ask those attending the thrift store for prayer requests. There were a couple of side glances at the pastor who had invited me. He shifted in his seat uncomfortably.

I asked one more question, "Do your teams ever invite people to church or give them cards that tell them about your churches?" The room got very strained at that point. The answer was no. I was not invited back to the leadership meeting.

My point is this: We are called to proclaim the gospel of Jesus Christ generously and graciously where we live, work, play, and also where we serve. These churches were doing a good work and a good service, but they had forgotten to share the gospel.

How easy would it have been to have a prayer request box with pen and paper handy? How easy would it have been to have cards inviting people to the church that was serving that week, placing them into bags as people were lealukeving? There were so many possibilities here and so many missed opportunities.

> "A sower went out to sow his seed. As he sowed, some seed fell along the path; it was trampled on, and the birds of the sky devoured it. Other seed fell on the rock; when it grew up, it with-

> ered away, since it lacked moisture. Other seed fell among thorns; the thorns grew up with it and choked it. Still other seed fell on good ground; when it grew up, it produced fruit: a hundred times what was sown." As he said this, he called out, "Let anyone who has ears to hear listen." (Luke 8:5–8)

As missional pastors we must take the posture from our heart, home, church, and community to show that we are sowers of the gospel each and every day. The sower had a workman mentality.

Main Points of the Passage:
1. The seed is the Word of God.
2. God has supplied you and I ample seed—His Word. That word is living and active.
3. The sower sowed his seed in full expectation that there would be a harvest.
4. Some seeds will be trampled on. Some seeds will wither away. Some seeds will be choked out by the busyness of life.
5. The seed that falls on good ground will bear much fruit.
6. Jesus invited us to listen, to reflect, and to put His message into practice in our missional pastorate.

Each and every day we need to sow the seed of the gospel as we go in hopeful expectation that some will come to faith.

Questions for Reflection:
1. Are you sowing the seed of the gospel where you live, work, and serve?
2. Are you trusting in the Word of God to lead people to faith, hope, and love in Jesus Christ?

3. Do you understand that some people will trample on the Word of God as you share it with them? If they did it to Jesus, they will do it to you.
4. Are you taking time to warn people who have received the gospel to beware of the busyness of life that can choke out the joy of the gospel?
5. Are you praying in expectation for good ground to sow the seed of the gospel?

When COVID-19 hit in full effect in 2020 and churches shut down, I was heartbroken like everyone else. We could not gather to worship, to serve, or to share the gospel. I was nearing the end of my time in Mobile, Alabama. Our campus ministries were shut down and our four summer mission trips were all cancelled.

I sat alone in my office in late February and was honestly angry that we could neither serve nor sow for the glory of God. I ripped up all the plans for my last few months and knelt to pray and asked, "How can I finish well if I am not allowed to?"

So, within a week, we went online with Monday, Wednesday, and Friday community groups that prayed together, shared our highs and lows, studied the Word of God, and prayed relentlessly for our community and our nation.

And, if you remember, COVID-19 was only the beginning of the storm. There was stock market meltdown, riots over the death of George Floyd, and a very turbulent presidential election.

It seemed each day was filled with bad news. So, I met with some friends through Zoom, and we created an online ministry platform that did four-to-five-minute gospel messages daily, as well as weekly online services. We called it Late Night Church.

We saturated our social media platforms with the gospel. When COVID-19 ended, we took that gospel saturation model to the inner cities of a midsize city and had tremendous results ministering to the truly less fortunate.

Practical Steps for Application:
1. Saturate your own heart with the gospel. Early morning and quiet times: Listen to preachers and teachers you respect when you work out or when you drive to work; pray and read Scripture to your family (without preaching at them).
2. Preach the gospel in your Sunday settings, teach the gospel in small group settings, and proclaim the gospel (four-to-six minutes) in service settings. I always utilize one passage each week and teach that across each platform.
3. Utilize your social media platforms to teach and preach the gospel each week. Again, keep it simple and focused. This should be a micro-sermon.
4. Celebrate those who come to faith and bear fruit! Celebrate it in your quiet time, with your family, church, and community. I am certain we do not celebrate our wins enough as Christians.
5. Create Bible study materials in reference to your weekly sermon and give them out each Sunday and encourage folks to study them and share them with those in their circle of life.

Why do we serve those in our care and why do we sow the gospel generously and graciously into their lives? So that they too may come in faith to Jesus Christ as their personal Lord and Savior. To God be the glory! Amen.

CHAPTER 4

Sacraments

Missional pastors intentionally, and through the leadership of the Holy Spirit, invite those in their care to place their faith in Jesus through the ordinances and sacraments of the church.

> "Therefore, everyone who hears these words of mine and acts on them will be like a wise man who built his house on the rock. The rain fell, the rivers rose, and the winds blew and pounded that house. Yet it didn't collapse, because its foundation was on the rock. (Matthew 7:24–25)

Missional Pastor Summation So Far:
Missional pastors live a life surrendered to the call of Jesus Christ; love and serve those Jesus has placed in their care; sow with generosity and grace the Word of God over those in their care; and, being led by the Holy Spirit, invite those in their care to faith in Jesus Christ and His Body through the sacraments (ordinances) of Holy Communion and Baptism.

In some Christian traditions, "sacrament" and "ordinance" are used to describe religious rites, but they differ in their theological emphasis. *Sacraments* are typically seen as means of grace, where

God actively bestows blessings upon participants. *Ordinances,* on the other hand, are viewed as symbolic acts commanded by Christ, demonstrating a believer's faith and obedience, rather than conferring grace.

Whether you are someone who sees Holy Communion and Baptism as sacramental or as an ordinance, I believe that they are tools that we can and should utilize under the leadership of the Holy Spirit to invite people to place their faith in Jesus Christ as Savior and Lord.

A missional pastor who is loving and who serves those in their care, and with great consistency sows the gospel over their lives, must plan that from time to time they must invite people to faith.

Sadly, I think there are many behind our pulpits each week who preach and teach the gospel but without the heartfelt expectation of making new disciples through an evangelistic invitation. I have witnessed this firsthand.

I was called to a wonderful church in Alabama to help rebuild its student ministry several years ago. This church had excellent facilities, two dynamically different worship services on Sunday mornings, a healthy and vibrant Sunday school and small group ministry, a thriving children's ministry, and tangible outreach to those on the margins. What it didn't have was a strong student ministry. There were many reasons for that, which I soon discovered.

My wife and I loved this church and its people. We still do.

However, there was one thing that didn't happen on Sundays. The people behind the pulpits would preach, teach, baptize children, and lead us in Holy Communion. However, they did not seize these beautiful, wonderful, gospel-centered opportunities to invite people to faith in Jesus Christ.

I could see it coming, the opportunity at the end of a message, the opportunity as we took time for Holy Communion, the opportunity as we baptized children. In all the times I was in these services, I may have seen it happen twice.

I brought it up several times how teaching, Holy Communion, and Baptism were natural segues to inviting people to faith. In my exit interview when I was leaving to move back to Tennessee, I brought it up as well. We had missed so many opportunities to lead people to faith.

Why did Jesus leave heaven and come to earth?

> **"For the Son of Man has come to seek and to save the lost." (Luke 19:10)**

I have witnessed the other side of this equation as well. When I was serving as associate pastor at a Baptist church in my wife's hometown, every single week they would extend an invitation and play song after song after song waiting for someone, anyone, to come forward.

Neither of these situations seemed to lean into the leadership of the Holy Spirit.

It's the Holy Spirit's job to convict people of their need for Christ as Savior and Lord, not ours.

There is this passage we recite when we offer Holy Communion in the Methodist Church, "Christ our Lord invites all to the table of Holy Communion who love Him, have earnestly repented of their sin, and who seek to live in peace with their brother and sister in Christ."

So—there it is. You shouldn't take Holy Communion if you don't love Jesus, have not repented of your sin, and are not living in peace with those around you.

I put Holy Communion at the end of our services on Sunday at our two urban churches. And, from time to time (every six to eight weeks), I would remind people that if they didn't love Christ, here was their opportunity to accept Him. I would simply walk through Billy Graham's prayer with them. Over a four-year period, we saw between two and three hundred men, women, and children (Black, white, and Hispanic) come to faith in Jesus

Christ as we sowed the gospel three to five times each week. We constantly offered them to faith in Christ as we paused to receive Holy Communion.

One hundred and sixty-five or more men, women, and children were baptized into the Body of Christ in rivers, cattle troughs, and baptisteries over that same period of time.

While sitting in a leadership meeting with local pastors, they wanted to know why and how we had seen so many come to faith and follow through in Baptism.

I shared our philosophy of ministry (which is what I am doing in this handbook). I also shared with them some of the stories of the men, women, and children who had come to faith over the last few years.

There was a large government-run apartment complex less than a mile from one of the churches we restarted. I prayer walked through the community several times and saw that there was no consistent gospel presence. So, we assembled a team and began to love and serve that community and share the gospel with them.

We also put together a children's ministry team and began to run a van over on Sunday afternoons. Before long we had a lot of single moms and their kids coming to church with us.

We began to do baptisms from time to time on the property (with a cattle trough) and at the church. One of the kids, who was always present at church and at the Village (that's what we called the apartment community), wanted to be baptized.

I took the time to explain we could definitely do that, but we would need to sit down and speak with his parents. I got his mother's phone number and called, but we never connected. Week after week, Jaquan would ask to be baptized. And, week after week, we reached out to his mom with no results.

We were going to have a great big block party in the Village one Wednesday and several parents and their kids were going to be baptized. Jaquan showed up, and his mom did as well. I sat down with his mother Kendra, and we talked about faith and Baptism. We then talked to Jaquan. He was so excited. Kendra agreed to allow Jaquan to be baptized (we never rebaptized people) as long as I would baptize her first! We did.

When Jaquan stepped into the cattle trough in front of a few hundred kids and parents in the Village, he was trembling with excitement. He had waited months for this moment.

When he came up out of the water, he threw his skinny arms in the air and flashed a great big smile. At that moment, one of our moms who was present snapped a picture of Jaquan and me. It was an amazing picture. I posted it on social media (with permission), and the picture went viral.

The baptism of Kendra and her son Jaquan led other moms, dads, and children to place their faith in Jesus Christ and to follow through in believers' baptism.

> **As they were eating, he took bread, blessed and broke it, gave it to them, and said, "Take it; this is my body." Then he took a cup, and after giving thanks, he gave it to them, and they all drank from it. He said to them, "This is my blood of the covenant, which is poured out for many. Truly I tell you, I will no longer drink of the fruit of the vine until that day when I drink it new in the kingdom of God." (The First Lord's Supper: Mark 14:22–26)**

> The eleven disciples traveled to Galilee, to the mountain where Jesus had directed them. When they saw him, they worshiped, but some doubted. Jesus came near and said to them, "All authority has been given to me in heaven and on earth. Go, therefore, and make disciples of all nations, baptizing them in the name of the Fa-

ther and of the Son and of the Holy Spirit, teaching them to observe everything I have commanded you. And remember, I am with you always, to the end of the age." (The Great Commission: Matthew 28:16–20)

Main Points of the Passage:
1. Jesus expected His disciples to gather together where He had directed them.
2. Jesus expected His disciples to partake in Holy Communion to remember His life, death, resurrection, and promised return.
3. Jesus expected His disciples to go and make disciples.
4. Jesus expected His disciples to teach them His Word and to baptize them into the Body of Christ.
5. Jesus promised to be with His disciples as they did so— The Holy Spirit.

Disciples who lean into Holy Communion and Baptism as part of the discipleship process will bear much fruit.

Questions for Reflection:
1. Are Holy Communion and Baptism a consistent part of your process of making new disciples?
2. Do you understand that Holy Communion is a holy moment that can lead people to faith, repentance, and reconciliation?
3. Do you see how someone being baptized can lead others in their circle of family and friends to want to place their faith in Jesus and be baptized as well?
4. What can you do in the next thirty to ninety days to make Holy Communion and Baptism a healthy part of your process of making new disciples?

Practical Steps for Application:
1. Consider making Holy Communion a weekly part of your service. You will need to trim down your sermon by five to ten minutes. But, it's worth it.
2. Every six to eight weeks, along with lots of prayer, allow the Holy Communion as part of your service to be used evangelistically.
3. Teach on believer's baptism the Sunday after you utilize Holy Communion in such a manner. Invite those who have never been baptized to sign up to do so. Maybe make it a river baptism!
4. Do not be afraid of sharing Holy Communion and Baptism in your outreach areas of ministry. Holy Communion and Baptism are missional elements of the church. Take them with you!

My last Sunday in Kentucky, before we moved to Tennessee for my wife to go to med school, we baptized fourteen men, women, and children down at the creek a few miles from our church.

As our lead pastor was baptizing these folks, a young mom in her late twenties approached me and asked if her mom and sister could be baptized as well.

These were not members of our church. They were a large family that was camping nearby and had been watching each child, student, and parent come forward to be baptized, and had heard their stories. They were inspired to place their faith in Jesus and be baptized as well. I waded out and told Pastor John. A few minutes later, the mom (mid-fifties) and her daughter (mid-thirties) waded out to him.

John spoke with them, prayed with them, and then baptized them! I got their names, phone numbers, and addresses. They lived in the town above ours, so I contacted a local church up there and encouraged them to reach out to this family of new believers.

Holy Communion and Baptism are tools of grace for the missional pastor to move people from hearing about Jesus to placing their faith in Him and becoming part of the family of God. Amen.

Chapter 5

Sent

Missional pastors send out those in their care each week to love and serve those in their care and to share the gospel generously and graciously with them.

> **And he himself gave some to be apostles, some prophets, some evangelists, some pastors and teachers, to equip the saints for the work of ministry. (Ephesians 4:11–12a)**

Missional Pastor Summation So Far:

Missional pastors live a life surrendered to the call of Jesus Christ; love and serve those Jesus has placed in their care; sow with generosity and grace the Word of God over those in their care; led by the Holy Spirit, invite those in their care to faith in Jesus Christ and His Body through the sacraments (ordinances) of Holy Communion and Baptism; and, with clarity, peace, and the words of Jesus, send them out to do likewise where they live, learn, work, and play.

In 1999, I was called to my wife's home church as the student ministry director. At one time it had been THE church to attend in her hometown and once had a thriving student ministry, which was led by the pastor who eventually led me to faith and into my calling. That church was a distant memory when I arrived. Some of the members remained from their heyday, but most had moved on to other churches.

I was tasked with rebuilding their youth group even though there were no longer families in the church who had students. The elderly members believed that a strong youth group would attract younger families. So, I did my best to do just that.

My first year there I had the privilege to attend a leadership conference in Gatlinburg, Tennessee, where pastoral leadership guru John Maxwell was going to be the main speaker. I purchased his latest book and got a chance to speak with him briefly as he signed autographs.

So, I quickly told him my story and where I was serving and the challenges we faced. He listened, nodded, and then quickly added, "Develop leaders and teams for the work of the ministry you've been called to, so they can carry on the ministry after you leave for the next assignment God has for you."

I went next door to the coffee shop and jotted down those words on the front page of his book. I don't remember the book I purchased (sorry John!), but I do remember what he told me. I had an expiration date, and I needed to leave the ministry with leaders and teams that would carry on the work of the ministry long after I departed.

So, I worked to do just that. We found leaders for our Sunday school classes and for our small group ministry (biweekly in-home meetings where we served a meal and where students led); we created a grandparent's ministry that connected all of our students with the older members of our congregation to give them a deeper connection; we found leaders for our ministry to the homeless. Then, when my time was drawing to a close, I gave the church a heads-up so they could find a quality youth ministry director to take my place. The ministry continued to thrive well after I departed.

However, not everyone is always willing to roll up their sleeves and grab hold of the ministry that God has so graciously placed into our hands. One member of another congregation heard my vision of developing leaders and teams for the work of the ministry and did not agree. She followed me back to my office and promptly told me that ministry was something "paid staff do, not church members."

Did I mention this was a committed church member, who was always available to help, and gave generously? She just didn't believe that *laity* (non-clergy) were qualified to be in leadership roles. No one had ever told her about the Priesthood of the Believers or that every Christ-follower was called, commanded, empowered, and equipped to make disciples.

So, I did. I asked her to sit down, and I shared some passages of Scripture with her, one of those being John 20:19–23.

The Disciples Commissioned

> When it was evening on that first day of the week, the disciples were gathered together with the doors locked because they feared the Jews. Jesus came, stood among them, and said to them, "Peace be with you." Having said this, he showed them his hands and his side. So, the disciples rejoiced when they saw the Lord. Jesus said to them again, "Peace be with you. As the Father has sent me, I also send you." After saying this, he breathed on them and said, "Receive the Holy Spirit. If you forgive the sins of any, they are forgiven them; if you retain the sins of any, they are retained." (John 20:19–23)

Main Points of the Passage:
1. Jesus blesses His followers with His peace. His peace is greater than any circumstances we can and will face in this life.
2. Jesus reveals Himself to His disciples and gives them evidence that it's really Him.
3. Jesus sends out His disciples just as the Father sent Jesus out. Why was He sent out? To seek and save the lost (Luke 19.10); to save and not condemn those who place their faith in Him (John 3:16–17).
4. Jesus gives His disciples the Holy Spirit to empower and equip them to do the work of the ministry.
5. Jesus gives His disciples authority. What are we to do with this authority? Love and serve (John 13:1–5).

With the rise of the professional pastor in the early part of the twentieth century, many church members felt the same way about ministry as this lady did, who was a strong and committed church member—that it is the role and responsibility of the pastor.

Jesus sent out all His disciples to live, love, and serve just like He did. That is what makes disciples the salt and light where we live, work, learn, and play.

Questions for Reflection:
1. Does your church understand that Jesus has called every disciple to the work of the ministry of making disciples, serving the less fortunate, and loving and serving those in their care as He did?
2. Do you understand that you have an expiration date? That one day your time will be up where you serve and that there needs to be leaders and teams to carry on the work that God has led you to begin?

3. Are you taking and making the time to train leaders and teams for the work of the ministry?
4. Are you and your leaders and teams leaning into the peace of Jesus, the Holy Spirit, and His authority to do the work of the ministry?
5. If you had to step away tomorrow from your current ministry, what would carry on and what would fall apart?
6. Without intentional leadership development of our laity, most likely none of our missional works will continue after our departure from our current ministry context.

Practical Steps for Application:
1. Set aside one day a week out of your schedule for leadership and team development.
2. Set aside lunch/breakfast on that day for leadership one-on-one development.
3. Set aside dinner on that day, at your home (if possible), for team development.
4. Make sure each leader and team has a clear job description along with expectations.
5. Pray with your leaders and your teams.

As part of your weekly sermon, end with a benediction that sends your people out to love and serve as Jesus loved and served and to share the gospel graciously and generously.

A few years ago, I planned a ten-day vacation to celebrate our thirtieth wedding anniversary. I planned this vacation about nine months beforehand so that I would have time to coordinate everything at both our urban churches and homeless ministries.

Two weeks out from our thirtieth anniversary vacation in early January, I could see that a massive cold front was going to be moving in. This cold front seemed to be lasting several days and was expected to hit while I was away.

So, I was proactive. I collaborated with both church councils and our ministry teams to ensure that all necessary logistics were in place.

About a week out, snow came into the forecast. I don't know if you've been in the South when it snows. We don't do well. Again, I was proactive. I went online to work on our social media, and thousands of dollars and supplies came in. As each day crept forward, it became increasingly clear that this was going to be a massive snowstorm. We needed to open warming centers for the homeless, a project that required the support of both our churches and the people of our community.

So, I made calls, went on TV, and everything went viral. People came from all over the community to help. The day the storm was supposed to hit our town was the same day I was to sail into the Caribbean for my anniversary trip.

Both church councils told my wife and I that Sunday to get in our car, drive to South Carolina, and get on our boat to enjoy our anniversary.

As we drove out of town that evening around 8:30 p.m., snow began to fall. And fall it did. Our town got smacked with between eight and twelve inches of snow that stayed on the ground for the next seven days, as temperatures did not rise above freezing that week.

One of our churches hosted over two hundred men, women, and children that week, while the other hosted seventy-five men, women, and children. And where was I? I was with my wife, in the Caribbean, celebrating our thirtieth anniversary. I kept in touch with them each morning and posted pictures and info on our social media pages. But the work of the ministry, a work that brought our churches local, state, national, and international attention, was done by laity, non-clergy men and women who had been sent by Jesus to do just that.

In February, we were contacted by the local atheist chapter. They told us that they appreciated our example of loving and serving the less fortunate and wanted to know if they could begin to serve and bring food on Sundays after our worship service to the homeless. We were blown away. They came and served and asked if they could serve the Easter meal because they knew how busy we were. They did. That evening on their social media page, they shared how they were a part of the Easter blessing to the homeless!

As missional pastors, part of our calling is to send people out to love and serve just like Jesus has sent us out to love and serve. And when they do, amazing things happen—for God's glory. Amen.

CHAPTER 6

Sincere

Missional pastors break bread with those in their care with joyful and sincere hearts.

> Now the entire group of those who believed were of one heart and mind, and no one claimed that any of his possessions was his own, but instead they held everything in common. With great power the apostles were giving testimony to the resurrection of the Lord Jesus, and great grace was on all of them. For there was not a needy person among them because all those who owned lands or houses sold them, brought the proceeds of what was sold, and laid them at the apostles' feet. This was then distributed to each person as any had need. (Acts 4:32–35)

Missional Pastor Summation So Far:

Missional pastors live a life surrendered to the call of Jesus Christ; love and serve those Jesus has placed in their care; sow with generosity and grace the Word of God over those in their care; led by the Holy Spirit, invite those in their care to faith in Jesus Christ and His Body through the sacraments (ordinances) of Holy Communion and Baptism; with clarity, peace, and the words of Jesus, send them out to do likewise where they live, learn, work, and play; and, break bread with those in their care with joyful and sincere hearts.

When you accept a call or an appointment to ministry in a local church and community, nothing can prepare you for the trouble or trauma that may be resonating in the hearts of those God has placed in your care.

I walked into this midsize church in the middle of a small town, as one of its two pastors. I didn't realize how much trauma and trouble the church had been through the previous couple of years.

One of their pastors had been inappropriate with church finances and with church members. The other pastor (the senior of the two) had resigned and moved about five miles down from the church and started a new one, which was a complete shock to the leadership of the church (the deacon board).

My co-pastor was a well-educated college professor who had originally been there as an interim, but eventually became the senior pastor, albeit part-time (he worked at a local Bible college).

In his own words—He preached there, I ministered. We worked well together.

On my first day there, I asked the secretary to print me a list of active members and the members who had left (it was estimated about half the membership had left over the previous twelve months). So, for my first thirty days in the office, Monday through Thursday, I called current members and those who had walked away. I asked questions, I listened, I listened some more, and then I prayed with them.

My call came as a surprise to current and previous members alike. My hope was to build trust, to build relationships, and to get our church moving forward.

Some of those I made phone calls with came down to the office to meet me face-to-face. One such member was a truck driver who drove down and took me to lunch. We hit it off well. We ate at the local Mexican restaurant, and he asked me questions. We're still friends to this day.

About a month or so after I started, I invited several of those folks to my home (the parsonage next door). That first Sunday evening after service we had about thirty people. The parsonage wasn't that big, so we used the back porch and the backyard to host everyone. Within a few weeks we were hosting upwards of fifty to seventy people on Sunday nights after service.

Pastor John reflected that Sunday that our people had a hunger to break bread together. They did, with joyful and sincere hearts.

We were at that church for little less than two years. In the second year we had over seventy baptisms, and one member (who happened to be a worldwide evangelist) said that he thought the church was as healthy as it had been in fifty years. On my final Sunday there, the church had a big meal where we broke bread again and our deacons gave me a $500 gift card to Home Depot to buy a new grill. They had accidentally caught mine on fire at a barbeque at my home and "melted it."

My wife and I have consistently opened our hearts and our home to those who have been placed in our care from the local church. Many times, more than I care to disclose, people have been surprised to be invited to the pastor's home.

When serving the homeless in Knoxville, I would sometimes bring those individuals I knew best to my home on cold afternoons and allow them to wash up, wash their clothes, and feed them a meal.

When those in our care see us opening our hearts and home to them, I think there is a bond that forms between pastor and church that is lasting, meaningful, and transformative.

> **Every day they devoted themselves to meeting together in the temple, and broke bread from**

> house to house. They ate their food with joyful and sincere hearts, praising God and enjoying the favor of all the people. Every day the Lord added to their number those who were being saved. (Acts 2:46–47)

Main Points of the Passage:
1. The Ancient Church were devoted to one another and to their leaders.
2. That devotion was reflected in their willingness to meet in one another's homes and break bread together with joy and sincere hearts.
3. The Ancient Church was filled with praise for God and was blessed with favor from their local community.
4. The Lord blessed them with healthy, vibrant church growth!

A pastor who opens his heart and home to break bread with those in his care will have a house filled with the joy and peace of the Lord.

Questions for Reflection:
1. Are you and the people in your church devoted to one another?
2. Do you open your heart and your home to break bread with those in your care?
3. Do you see the favor of God in your local community?
4. Are you and your people filled with the praise of God?
5. Is the Lord adding to your church through the salvation of others?

The world is filled with lonely people who are hungry for true community. When we open our hearts and homes to those in our care, we model true, Christ-centered community. It's contagious.

Practical Steps for Application:
1. Open your heart and your home monthly to your leaders.
2. Open your heart and your home bimonthly to your members.
3. Open your heart and your home semiannually to new members.
4. You make the main dish, and ask those who are invited to fill out the rest of the menu.
5. And, although I've already covered this, open your heart and your home to your neighbors.

At one of our leadership dinners as we all sat down to dinner, I asked a question. The question was, "Where do you see God at work in your life and where do you need God to work in your life?"

There were about fifteen of us around the dinner table (I have a BIG table just for occasions like this). Now, let me just say that I know everyone at the table. They are my friends. I pray with them weekly (that's another chapter).

But this question was to open the eyes and the hearts of those around the table. Two of the leaders at the table were husband and wife and I knew they were struggling. However, that wasn't for me to disclose. When it got to the wife, she talked about the needs of her kids. When it got to her husband, a great big guy with an even bigger heart, he looked down at the table and then spoke truth. "I need God to work on my marriage," he said. Silence.

In that moment, without revealing any drama, he told our team he and his wife needed some real prayer.

When we break bread with one another, God can do some good work. Amen.

I am thankful to say that couple is doing just fine. Praise God!

CHAPTER 7

Sheep

Missional pastors partner with those in their care to feed the hungry, clothe the naked, house the homeless, care for the sick, and visit the imprisoned.

> "Then he will also say to those on the left, 'Depart from me, you who are cursed, into the eternal fire prepared for the devil and his angels! For I was hungry and you gave me nothing to eat; I was thirsty and you gave me nothing to drink; I was a stranger and you didn't take me in; I was naked and you didn't clothe me, sick and in prison and you didn't take care of me.' (The Words of Jesus: Matthew 25:41–43)

Missional Pastor Summation So Far:

Missional pastors live a life surrendered to the call of Jesus Christ; love and serve those Jesus has placed in their care; sow with generosity and grace the Word of God over those in their care; led by the Holy Spirit, invite those in their care to faith in Jesus Christ and His Body through the sacraments (ordinances) of Holy Communion and Baptism; with clarity, peace, and the words of Jesus, send them out to do likewise where they live, learn, work, and play; break bread with those in their care with joyful and sincere hearts; and, with those in their care, feed the hungry, clothe the naked, house the homeless, care for the sick, and visit the imprisoned.

As the director of a student ministry in 1999 at a local church in East Tennessee, we were creating a strong, relational ministry that was biblically accurate and culturally relevant. This meant that our kids were grounded in the Word, in prayer, and in relationship to the Body of Christ, and they were carrying their faith to their peers on their campuses.

There was a growing ministry to the homeless in the Knoxville area, and they were constantly on the local Christian radio stations asking for volunteers. One day, I gave the ministry a call and was able to speak with the person who had started it. I told him that I wanted our students (and my kids) to come that November and December to volunteer every weekend during the holidays.

He thanked me and then got real. He told me that he had plenty of volunteers for the holidays, that he really needed volunteers from January to October. That struck a chord. So, I spoke with my wife and our volunteer team. We all agreed that we would serve the last Sunday of each month, whenever we had in-service days (students would be out of school while teachers got caught up), and then one day every week during the summer.

I remember the first Sunday when we prepared the meal for dinner and then traveled over in two church vans and a couple of SUVs. When we arrived, there was a large station wagon parked next to the shelter with a family sitting in it. It was obvious that they were living out of their car.

When we all began to get out and grab our food and other items, the family got out of their car as well. There was a little girl that got out of the station wagon; she was about six years old, with long curly brown hair.

"Are you here to feed us?" she asked. Our hearts melted. "Yes," one of our students said. We went inside and did just that. Our students served the meal. Several of them, along with our adult volunteers, sat with the sixty or seventy men, women, and children who came for the meal. They were all homeless, and each of them had a story. We prayed over them, shared the gospel with them, and loved them as best we could.

From 1999 to 2013, we took student groups from that church and my next two churches to Knox Area Rescue Ministry to serve. It was always a meaningful experience to feed the hungry, to build relationships with them, to pray with them and to share faith, hope, and the love of Christ with them. My own children loved to serve as well, and some of their best memories of their youth group were at KARM.

In 2021, I was appointed to two closed and condemned churches in urban areas of Knoxville, Tennessee, and was asked to get them back open again.

The first few weeks I was there I read everything I could about these two once-vibrant, blue-collar churches. In reading their histories, it was obvious that when the communities around both churches changed, the churches did not.

They went inside their church buildings and shut their doors to the opportunity to be a powerful and present witness for Christ to the needy that were now in their neighborhoods. The result: They became irrelevant in their neighborhood and eventually died.

We made caring for the hungry, the homeless, the sick, the widowed, the orphaned, and those returning home from prison our priority. Let me be clear, it wasn't easy. It was work. In fact, it was labor that demanded heart, mind, soul, and strength. It definitely commanded a vibrant, Christ-centered community to do so.

We had discussions and disagreements along the way about how to best go about this and how to keep Jesus at the center of it all. I constantly reminded people that we were not the local rescue ministry, we were a local church; and, a local church's mission was not only to care for the less fortunate, but to make disciples. And we did.

> When the Son of Man comes in his glory, and all the angels with him, then he will sit on his glorious throne. . . . Then the King will say to those on his right, "Come, you who are blessed by my Father; inherit the kingdom prepared for you from the foundation of the world. For I was hungry and you gave me something to eat; I was thirsty and you gave me something to drink; I was a stranger and you took me in; I was naked and you clothed me; I was sick and you took care of me; I was in prison and you visited me." Then the righteous will answer him, "Lord, when did we see you hungry and feed you, or thirsty and give you something to drink? When did we see you a stranger and take you in, or without clothes and clothe you? When did we see you sick, or in prison, and visit you?" And the King will answer them, "Truly I tell you, whatever you did for one of the least of these brothers and sisters of mine, you did for me." (Matthew 25:31, 34–40)

Main Points of the Passage:
1. Jesus is coming back. We need to be prepared to give a good account of the life and ministry He has entrusted to us.
2. Jesus will reward exceedingly and abundantly those who have cared for the less fortunate.
3. The least of these should be a priority of the local church.
4. We are to engage the less fortunate as if they were Jesus.

5. Those who do not prioritize the less fortunate should be prepared to give an account to Jesus as to why they did not do so.

When the snowstorm hit in 2024, our two churches and one other opened their doors to the less fortunate. That snow stayed on the ground for more than a week. For that week, the temperature never rose above freezing. We have several megachurches in our city, and they were silent—deafeningly so—during this seven-to-ten-day stretch

One local pastor approached me and expressed his anger that no one had asked him to open his church for the less fortunate to come out of the cold.

No one asked us to open our doors. We knew our community, our neighborhood, and our neighbors. We knew they would not only need a warm place for sleep but also hot meals.

I kindly told the pastor he didn't need to ask for permission to be the local church. He needed to get to know his neighborhood so that when the cold came back again, he and his church would know what to do.

Questions for Reflection:
1. Are you and your church prepared for the return of Jesus?
2. Do you believe that you could give a good account of your church for its care of the marginalized?
3. Where are the hungry, the homeless, and those on the margins in the neighborhood around your church? What are you and your church doing to engage them with the love of Christ and tangible ministry?
4. Who will be a gospel witness to those in your community on the margins if you're not willing or able to?
5. When you see those on the margins of life in your community, do you see them as Jesus? We must, or we will never move like we need to.

Practical Steps for Application:
1. Pray that God would give you and your church eyes to see the less fortunate as if they were Jesus.
2. Pray that God would give you and your church a love for the less fortunate in your community, like they were Jesus.
3. Look for practical, meaningful ways you can meet the needs of the hungry and homeless men, women, and children who are less fortunate in your community.
4. Plan, organize, and communicate the ministry you are going to conduct for the less fortunate to your family and church family. Invite everyone to get involved.
5. Do this with remarkable consistency, care, and always share generously and graciously the gospel of Jesus Christ.

One of our urban churches had a *parsonage* (a home that churches would assign to their lead pastor). We flipped that parsonage into a home for homeless young women aged between eighteen and twenty-four years old. We helped them with their education (GED/high school diploma), job training and jobs, gaining life skills, health care, and more.

There were expectations. They had to pay a weekly participation fee; they had to help volunteer at the church to serve the less fortunate; they had to keep their rooms clean and their home in order.

Several of our leaders grew up homeless, so we had an understanding of what would be helpful expectations for the young women to have each week.

It was messy, hard work. But it was so worth it. We took young, at-risk young women off the streets and gave them a home and a faith family.

Our community leaders rallied around Hope House. Hope House, like our congregation, was mutiracial in its makeup. I believe it was and is a powerful witness of what the Body of Christ can do when it sees the less fortunate like Jesus and has a healthy sense of urgency to do something to help.

So, find the less fortunate around your home and your church, and be on mission with God to engage them and love and serve them, so that when Jesus returns you can give a good account of the life and ministry Jesus blessed you with. Amen!

CHAPTER 8

Skilled Master Builder

Missional pastors are skilled at laying foundational ministries for those who will come after them.

> So I said to them, "You see the trouble we are in. Jerusalem lies in ruins and its gates have been burned. Come, let's rebuild Jerusalem's wall, so that we will no longer be a disgrace." I told them how the gracious hand of my God had been on me, and what the king had said to me. They said, "Let's start rebuilding," and their hands were strengthened to do this good work. (Nehemiah 2:17–18)

Missional Pastor Summation So Far:
Missional pastors live a life surrendered to the call of Jesus Christ; love and serve those Jesus has placed in their care; sow with generosity and grace the Word of God over those in their care; led by the Holy Spirit, invite those in their care to faith in Jesus Christ and His Body through the sacraments (ordinances) of Holy Communion and Baptism; with clarity, peace, and the words of Jesus, send them out to do likewise where they live, learn, work, and play; break bread with those in their care with

joyful and sincere hearts; with those in their care, feed the hungry, clothe the naked, house the homeless, care for the sick, and visit the imprisoned; and, are skilled at laying foundational ministries for those who will come after them.

In Johnson City, Tennessee, I had the wonderful privilege of working with the Holston Baptist Association, the Tennessee Baptist Convention, and the North American Mission Board to plant (*replant*, some would call it) a neighborhood church. We started with about ten committed individuals and ended with a healthy local church of about one hundred and fifty men, women, and children—the majority of which were either unchurched or had walked away from church.

We hosted more than twenty-five mission teams over four summers to engage our community, and to spread the gospel of Jesus Christ. To God be the glory!

When our time was over there, we were expecting to move to Greenville, North Carolina, for my wife to serve her medical residency (her calling in Christ). But as often happens, God threw us a curveball.

On Match Day (that's when medical students are told where they will attend residency) in April of 2016, she was informed that instead of North Carolina, we would be moving to Mobile, Alabama. We were stunned and greatly disappointed. In anticipation of the move to North Carolina, I had already interviewed and been hired by a midsize church of about five hundred to care for their children, students, and families. So, after the Match Day luncheon, I had to make that call to tell them that we would not be moving.

The senior pastor took it in stride and encouraged me that God was at work in this process and to look and see where He was at work in Mobile and join Him there.

A couple of weeks later, my wife and I were in Mobile to look at the campus where she would be doing residency, the city, and the homes. I also reached out to the Alabama Baptist Convention, the local association office (multiple times), and local churches that were looking for a pastor. Can I just say that none of those doors ever opened for me in Mobile?

So, I looked to see what jobs were available in Mobile. The first one that popped up was at a large United Methodist Church. So, I sent them my resume. Within a few days I was talking with them and was then hired by them to rebuild their student ministry.

They interviewed more than twenty people over an eighteen-month period. None of them panned out. Dauphin Way was a very well-known church with an amazing staff, thriving worship services, healthy small groups and Sunday school, a dynamic children's ministry, and a successful outreach ministry. But, it had not had a strong student ministry in over thirty years according to the men and women who served there and called Dauphin Way home.

Their student ministry area was in the basement and was constantly flooding (the city was under sea level). I was asked by one of the senior pastors if I could be happy with ten students. Ten? This was a church of fifteen hundred members and six to seven hundred folks on Sundays. I thought we could do better than ten.

By the end of our first summer there, I came up with a purpose statement that I would focus on our entire time at Dauphin Way. Our purpose: to partner with parents and to make disciples of students who loved and serves God, one another, and the less fortunate.

We did just that. We had an extra room built onto the back of our small home just to host parents and volunteers (the overwhelming majority of our volunteers were parents). Two or three times each month we would host dinners with parents. One would be for middle school parents, one for high school parents. This built a deep sense of community and purpose.

We prayed with these parents. We loved, encouraged, and supported these parents from day one until our final days at Dauphin Way UMC.

One of my weekly habits is to send prayer notes out to those in my care. Normally, I just send a simple text: *"How can I pray for you today?"* Since I purchased my first cell phone in 2001, I've done this, normally on Tuesdays. I can tell you the first time someone in my circle of life gets that message their response is pretty generic—such as, *"Pray for me and my family."* But the longer they get these simple messages, the more real they get.

During our final week at Dauphin Way, one parent asked if I would continue to send those notes. I did for a short time.

We built a campus ministry for the public and private schools that our middle and high school students were attending. Lunchtime on Mondays, Tuesdays, and Wednesdays, I found myself on campuses building relationships with our students (my kids too!) and their peers. We hosted outreach events like lock-ins, Super Bowl gatherings, school kickoffs, and more to connect our students and their peers and families to one another.

We built worship services, small groups, and multiple summer mission trips for our students who were very committed, as well as those who were casual attenders.

And, in the end, instead of hiring someone from outside of our church to replace me when my family moved back to Tennessee after my wife's medical residency, the church chose an amazing individual who had helped love, care, and serve our students and families for the entire time we were there.

I am so very pleased to say that this person took the foundations we had laid and built an even stronger student ministry!

> **According to God's grace that was given to me, I have laid a foundation as a skilled master builder, and another builds on it. But each one is to be careful how he builds on it. For no one can lay**

any foundation other than what has been laid down. That foundation is Jesus Christ. (1 Corinthians 3:10–11)

Main Points of the Passage:
1. Paul and Nehemiah recognized that God had given them grace.
2. Paul and Nehemiah recognized that God had given that grace with and for a purpose.
3. Paul and Nehemiah rolled up their sleeves and went to work laying foundations with that grace.
4. Paul and Nehemiah worked with and through those around them to accomplish the work God had placed in their hands.
5. Paul recognized that Jesus was and is the proper foundation of all our work.

Questions for Reflection:
1. Do you recognize the grace that God has given you?
2. Do you recognize the purpose of the grace that God has given you?
3. Are you, like Paul and Nehemiah, rolling up your sleeves to lay that foundation for the leaders that are to come after you?
4. Are you inviting others to partner with you to accomplish this God-given purpose?
5. Like Paul, do you recognize that the foundation is Jesus Christ? And do we need to keep him at the forefront of our purpose always?

Practical Steps for Application:
1. Know where you are going. Nehemiah was given God's favor to rebuild Jerusalem's walls; Paul was given God's favor to plant churches. Why has God put you where you

are? What is your distinctive contribution? Keep that vision before you at all times.
2. Become a skilled master builder at what He has called you to be and do. Continuously improve. Increase your capabilities. Be a constant learner.
3. Invite others to join you on the journey. Make sure they understand where you're going, what is expected of them, and the grace God has given you to make things happen.
4. Deliver results. Get the right things done. Make things happen. Accomplish what God has called you to do.
5. Practice accountability. Hold yourself accountable first to your calling; hold others accountable second. Don't point fingers or blame others when things go wrong (trust me, from time to time, things will go wrong).

The team and ministry that we built at Dauphin Way was light-years ahead of the ministry we had built twenty years previously. And the ministries we build moving forward I hope will be even better.

In 2021, I became good friends with an individual who had been deeply hurt by church many, many years ago. He wasn't bitter, he was still wounded. As I painted our new kid's ministry rooms, he told me his story and shed tears.

God had an obvious call on his life, and he had lived out that call outside the four walls of the local church. For all practical purposes, he was the pastor in the community around the church we were about to reopen on Easter.

So, he became my primary partner in that community and in our new local church. I am deeply thankful to say that he was licensed as a local pastor by our Conference last year and he was the pastor who was appointed to take my place when I stepped away this past spring.

Pastors, we all have an expiration date. When we accept a call or an appointment, we need to lay a strong foundation of leaders and teams for the work of the ministry. If we do not, when we leave, things will collapse.

Chapter 9

Steadfast

Missional pastors are steadfast in the Lord's work, because they know their labors are not in vain.

> I am sure of this, that he who started a good work in you will carry it on to completion until the day of Christ Jesus. (Philippians 1:6)

Missional Pastor Summation So Far:

Missional pastors live a life surrendered to the call of Jesus Christ; love and serve those Jesus has placed in their care; sow with generosity and grace the Word of God over those in their care; led by the Holy Spirit, invite those in their care to faith in Jesus Christ and His Body through the sacraments (ordinances) of Holy Communion and Baptism; with clarity, peace, and the words of Jesus, send them out to do likewise where they live, learn, work, and play; break bread with those in their care with joyful and sincere hearts; with those in their care, feed the hungry, clothe the naked, house the homeless, care for the sick, and visit the imprisoned; are skilled at laying foundational ministries for those who will come after them; and, are steadfast in the Lord's work, because they know their labors are not in vain.

In the late nineties, my wife and I were trying to have a baby. We had suffered miscarriage after miscarriage after miscarriage. Five in all, the final being twins. It devastated my wife. It was during this time that we had started going to church, placed our faith in Jesus Christ, and truly began to live for the Lord.

We prayerfully decided to try one more time before my wife enrolled in nursing school at the local university. So, we came to church that Wednesday evening and asked the core group of our growing, vibrant church to pray with us and for us that we would be successful this time in having a baby.

There were about fifty to sixty people there that night. The pastor called us forward, and one by one, everyone in the church that night came to surround us and pray over us. We cried. They cried. It was a balm to the soul of my wife. One of the elderly members there grabbed my hand, looked me in the eye, and said, "You'll get your baby."

Six weeks later, we were pregnant. A couple of months later, we had a scary moment where we thought she was going to have another miscarriage. We rushed to the doctor's office, and they did an ultrasound.

That was when we heard this beautiful sound of a fast-beating heart. My wife and I burst into tears. They nurse said, "It's okay!" And we replied, "We know it is."

A week before her due date, my wife's water broke, and we made our way to the hospital. Now, the plan was to have the baby naturally. But, once those real labor pains set in, my wife quickly changed her mind and asked for the epidural. But even with the epidural, she still had to labor to give birth.

Several hours later, with a lot of blood, sweat, and tears, she gave birth to an eight-pound-five-ounce baby girl. She was our little miracle baby.

If we want to see our hearts, homes, churches, and communities transformed, it's going to take steadfast labor.

This past winter in our community was an especially long, cold, hard winter. It began at the beginning of December and continued throughout March. I was constantly looking at the extended forecast to make sure we were ahead of the curve when it came to planning, organizing leadership, and management.

Our frontline management people were men and women who had formerly been homeless. They stayed at the shelters around the clock during each cold spell. When the temperatures dropped below freezing, our doors opened. When it snowed, our doors opened. We had cots, blankets, pillows, warm clothing, and hot meals.

Our leadership personnel were men and women who were on our church councils and lead teams. We divided our shifts in half around the clock. I would normally roll in at 6 a.m. and check on both shelters. Then I would go to make purchases and let the world know on social media what our needs were that day.

It worked. All in all, hundreds of men, women, and children were taken off the streets and into our churches to be loved, fed, and given a place to rest and sleep.

Donations—financial, food, clothing, etc.—rolled in day and night. Several times we just told people we didn't need anything else. Our cup runneth over.

But it was work, it was labor, and it was at times physically, mentally, spiritually, and relationally exhausting. But we did it! Each day, our team rolled up their sleeves and were steadfast in their love and devotion to serve the least of these.

> **Therefore, my dear brothers and sisters, be steadfast, immovable, always excelling in the Lord's work, because you know that your labor in the Lord is not in vain. (1 Corinthians 15:58)**

Main Points of the Passage:
1. Missional pastors and churches are to be steadfast in their labor in the Lord.
2. Missional pastors and churches are to be immovable in their labor in the Lord.
3. Missional pastors and churches are to excel in the Lord's work.
4. Our work and labor in the Lord are never in vain.
5. Quitting is not an option for missional pastors and churches.

There have been times when I wanted to quit. Once in 2015, I was exhausted. But, my wife told me my labor in Johnson City wasn't done yet. The next day, I received a book in the mail from NAMB; the name of the book? *Don't Quit Before You Finish*. That was all it took to keep my focus and labor going.

Questions for Reflection:
1. Are you and your church steadfast in the work you have been given by the Lord?
2. Are you and your church immovable in the work the Lord has assigned you?
3. Are you and your church excelling in the work the Lord has assigned you?
4. Do you and your church realize that your work and labor in the Lord is not in vain?
5. Do you and your church realize that your labor will produce good fruit for the Lord's glory?

From time to time, we as missional pastors will need to remind everyone why we do what we do and why it's so important that we do it. That's our job.

Practical Steps for Application:
1. Decide in your heart, mind, and soul that you will not quit the Lord's work.
2. Decide you will be steadfast and immovable in the Lord's work.
3. Decide that you will seek to excel in the Lord's work.
4. Make it a point in your team meetings and church council meetings to remind everyone of the work the Lord has called your church to do and encourage them to be steadfast, immovable, and to excel in it.
5. Give thanks for the work the Lord has called you to daily.

On my last day at one of our churches in Knoxville, we baptized thirteen people. A dad and his two sons; a mom and her entire family; a homeless man who once struggled with addiction, now clean and with a home to call his own; and, a single mom and her two babies. Hallelujah! At the homeless shelter that same week, I was able to invite people to faith, share Holy Communion with them, and baptize many more. To God be the glory!

We finished well—steadfast, immovable, and excelling in the Lord's work. Amen.

CHAPTER 10

The Samaritan's Purse

Missional pastors seek to do everything in love.

> Be alert, stand firm in the faith, be courageous, be strong. Do everything in love. (1 Corinthians 16:13–14)

Final Missional Pastor Summation:
Missional pastors live a life surrendered to the call of Jesus Christ; love and serve those Jesus has placed in their care; sow with generosity and grace the Word of God over those in their care; led by the Holy Spirit, invite those in their care to faith in Jesus Christ and His Body through the sacraments (ordinances) of Holy Communion and Baptism; with clarity, peace, and the words of Jesus, send them out to do likewise where they live, learn, work, and play; they break bread with those in their care with joyful and sincere hearts; with those in their care, they feed the hungry, clothe the naked, house the homeless, care for the sick, and visit the imprisoned; are skilled at laying foundational ministries for those who will come after them; are steadfast in

the Lord's work, because they know their labors are not in vain; and, seek to do everything in love.

The Apostle Peter said to the early church, "**Above all, love each other deeply, because love covers over a multitude of sins." (1 Peter 4:8)**

I planted a church in the early 2000s with a good friend. We were one of the first churches that utilized dynamic, contemporary worship music in our morning services. Gone were the hymnals, the organs, and the choirs. In came amps, guitars, drums, sound systems, and rock-and-roll stars for Jesus! Our service was very loud, but in a good way.

From the moment we launched our church plant in a local high school, we had a crowd. The church plant was so popular that it eventually went multisite and multicounty.

But it was clear from early on that my vision of what the church was and would become and the vision of my partner was very different. Very different.

One of us saw church as a process. The other—a program, maybe even a product to be consumed. For me, programs entertain, but they do not transform us into the people of God. And, to be honest, consumer Christianity was the BIG thing in the 1990s and early 2000s. People would flock to large churches and consume worship and messages, then rush back out and their lives looked no different from the world around them.

This person I planted this church with began to annoy me, to get under my skin. Before I realized it, I really didn't like this individual who had once been a very good friend and partner in ministry.

Then we began to argue, sometimes even in front of the other team members. Things were not going well. I didn't like myself because I was becoming a very angry pastor. Our world doesn't need angry pastors.

We had an elder meeting coming up and it was my turn to lead the devotion. Many of the elders knew about the tension between us. One of them even called me and asked me what I was going to do at the meeting. Would I split this new church? Would I cause division? Would I openly begin to share with others my disagreements?

I sincerely believe that the church is the Bride of Christ. As pastors and leaders, our attitudes and actions should never, ever hurt the church.

So, I prayed, I fasted, and I found my answer in John 13.

I sat a gallon of water, a basin, and some towels in the room we were going to have our meeting in the night before. That Saturday morning almost twenty-five years ago, I led the devotion. I then confessed my negative attitude towards my friend, asked for forgiveness, and then I washed his feet.

The leader who had called me the day before called me again later that Saturday to let me know how thankful he was with what had transpired that morning.

Our service to our family, to our church, and to our community must be grounded in love and led by love.

We must preach the gospel with love for our church. We must love to make fully devoted followers of Christ out of those placed in our care. We must love to shepherd those in our care. We must love to invest in and redeem the less fortunate in our community. We must love to develop leaders and teams for the work of the community. When I was in Mobile, Alabama, I would park my car as far away from our church as I could and then, as I walked from my car to the building, I would pray a prayer of thanksgiving for each of our staff members.

Then, I would take extra time to stop by and see each of them as often as I could—either on the way in or the way out. It helped to develop within me a deep sense of thanksgiving, gratitude, and love for those men and women I worked with each day.

My final week there in Mobile was during COVID-19. The church was not allowed to officially gather under our state and federal guidelines.

But the staff (nonpastoral) of twenty gathered, shared a meal, and then offered to pray over me (from a safe distance). One of the staff members said that she could not pray for me from a distance, so she walked over and placed her hands on my back and began to pray. Then the other staff members did as well. I wept.

Love will bind our marriages, our families, our churches, and our communities together.

> **Then an expert in the law stood up to test him, saying, "Teacher, what must I do to inherit eternal life?" "What is written in the law?" he asked him. "How do you read it?" He answered, "Love the Lord your God with all your heart, with all your soul, with all your strength, and with all your mind," and "your neighbor as yourself." "You've answered correctly," he told him. "Do this and you will live." But wanting to justify himself, he asked Jesus, "And who is my neighbor?" Jesus took up the question and said, "A man was going down from Jerusalem to Jericho and fell into the hands of robbers. They stripped him, beat him up, and fled, leaving him half dead. A priest happened to be going down that road. When he saw him, he passed by on the other side. In the same way, a Levite, when he arrived at the place and saw him, passed by on the other side. But a Samaritan on his journey came up to him, and when he saw the man, he had compassion. He went over to him and bandaged his wounds, pouring on olive oil and wine. Then he put him on his own animal, brought**

> him to an inn, and took care of him. The next day he took out two denarii, gave them to the innkeeper, and said, 'Take care of him. When I come back I'll reimburse you for whatever extra you spend.' Which of these three do you think proved to be a neighbor to the man who fell into the hands of the robbers? The one who showed mercy to him," he said. Then Jesus told him, "Go and do the same." (Luke 10:25–37)

Main Points of the Passage:
1. The key to eternal life is to love God with our all.
2. The key to eternal life is to love our neighbor as ourselves.
3. The key to eternal life is to show compassion to the less fortunate.
4. Showing compassion to the less fortunate may be costly, but Jesus promises to reward us abundantly and eternally.
5. Those who fail to show compassion to the less fortunate are not being led by the love of Christ and will miss out on His abundant and eternal life.

Questions for Reflection:
1. Why does God require us to love Him?
2. Why does God require us to love our neighbor?
3. Why is the story of the Good Samaritan such a powerful example of love and compassion in action?
4. Why do you think the Levite and the priest went around the man and avoided showing him compassion?
5. Who in your life do you need to extend compassion to, like the Samaritan?

This passage strikes me hard because I know how busy we can become with church work. Sometimes we are so exhausted and so busy with church work that we are empty of compassion and grace when we encounter genuine need.

Practical Steps for Application:
1. Pray each day to love God with all your heart.
2. Pray each day to love those in your care with all your heart.
3. Pray each day for love and compassion for the less fortunate you will encounter that day.
4. Move from prayer to action in your love for God, one another, and the less fortunate.

I have, over the last several years, geared my days around loving service to my wife, my kids, my church, and the less fortunate in our community. But, there are still days when I encounter difficult and sinful people, and love and compassion are not the first things on my mind or in my heart.

Then the Holy Spirit reminds me that I, too, am quite difficult and sinful, and He loves me anyway. So, I back up and try again to do everything in love.

When I began my journey in ministry several years ago, I met with a representative from the local church. About half an hour into coffee together, they shared all the mess in their life. At that moment, I could have walked around the mess, shaken my head, and said a trite prayer. The Holy Spirit spoke to me, telling me I could judge them or love them. I chose to love them and walk beside them as their pastor.

If we don't love the people in our care, nothing else will work. Love is the reason our Heavenly Father sent His Son, Jesus. Love is the reason Jesus sends us into the world to be missional pastors. Love can and should be the defining characteristic of our lives, marriages, families, and local churches. When love defines us, it will define those around us as well.

So, may you go and love well all those God has placed in your care today, tomorrow, and until the return of Jesus Christ. Amen.

It is my sincere belief that if a local pastor prayerfully and wisely applies these biblical principles and practical steps to life and ministry each week, they will bear much fruit, bring glory to God, and prove themselves to be fully devoted followers of Jesus Christ.

Epilogue:

In early 2025, I realized that my heart and soul were tired—tired from the heavy toll of ministry on the front lines of COVID-19 and homelessness over the last five years; tired of the politics that had somehow taken centerstage when it came to our ministry to the homeless; tired of wrestling with leaders who didn't understand why ministry to the less fortunate should be so crucial to Christ-followers and local churches.

My soul lamented the plight of the homeless in our community. I grieved to see a city so wealthy and yet so indifferent to their fellow man. Like a soldier who had been in the trenches for too long, I needed an extended break before I was broken—or worse, disillusioned. So, after much prayer and many discussions with my wife, I awaited a call from my district superintendent. A few days later, while in a meeting, I received a text message from them. During that call, I expressed how tired my heart and soul were and the need I had for an extended break. After many more discussions, I received one.

Many people didn't understand why I asked to step away. So, I took the time to explain why I did privately. I wasn't burned out, but I was on the path to it without a much-needed sabbatical.

Pastoral burnout is real. According to a recent study, 65% of pastors are currently experiencing burnout in their ministry, and 42% of pastors were considering leaving full-time ministry altogether.

Pastoral burnout is defined as *the moment or season when a pastor loses the motivation, hope, energy, joy, and focus required to fulfill his work, and these losses center on the work itself.*

In these last few pages, I want to extend a few strong, practical encouragements that have helped me to maintain my physical and mental health, keep me accountable, and retain a missional focus.

Missional pastors need sleep.

> Unless the Lord builds a house, its builders labor over it in vain; Unless the Lord watches over a city, the guard stays alert in vain. In vain you get up early and stay up late, working hard to have enough food— Yes, he gives sleep to the one he loves. (Psalm 127:1–2)

I cannot express the importance of getting a consistent good night's sleep. You will not excel in your life or ministry if you do not.

The National Institute of Health lists these issues for those who consistently do not get a good night's sleep. Sleep deficiency is linked to many chronic health problems, including heart disease, kidney disease, high blood pressure, diabetes, stroke, obesity, and depression.

The physical and mental benefits of a consistent good night's sleep are innumerable: improved memory, focus, and learning; better mood and emotional health; increased energy and alertness; stronger immune system; reduced risk of chronic diseases such as heart disease and diabetes. Those are just a few benefits that you can find in a quick Internet search.

John Wesley, the founder of Methodism, encouraged his followers to go to bed and to get up at the same time, creating a healthy circadian rhythm for life and ministry. In his sermon, "The Most Excellent Way," he encouraged his listeners to take as much sleep as they needed.

To be a healthy missional pastor, determine your ideal sleep amount and set a daily bedtime and wake-up time. Stick to it. If you do, the benefits of a good night's sleep will help you maintain physical and mental health. I go to bed at around 9 p.m. each night and wake up by 4 a.m. each morning. This has kept me physically and mentally fit.

I usually allow myself to sleep in on my Sabbath day, but that is another point altogether.

Missional pastors need physical strength.

> For physical training is of some value, but godliness has value for all things, holding promise for both the present life and the life to come. (1 Timothy 4:8 NIV)

When I was in Kentucky, we constantly used food as a hook to get people to youth and adult functions. It worked. It was a small town (think Mayberry), and people loved gathering together around a cookout.

One Fourth of July, we had a massive block party and invited the entire community around the church to join us. They showed up! Over twenty different homemade ice cream makers were churning, multiple grills were cooking hot dogs and hamburgers, and everyone wanted me to taste their signature side item. Of course, I had to taste them!

That night, my youngest son crawled up in my lap, patted my belly, and told me that he "loved his little fat daddy." He was four and adorable, but that truth opened my eyes to all the weight I had gained that year. I got on the scale and realized I was more than forty pounds overweight.

The next day, I began to take brisk two-mile walks to exercise, and I went on a keto diet (think meats, vegetables, eggs, and dairy). A year later, I had lost those forty pounds and felt much better, and my son never again called me his little fat daddy.

Our nation and our local churches are overweight and obese. Heart disease and diabetes are just two of the most widely known negatives when it comes to being overweight.

Missional pastors need to pursue godliness, but we also need to take better care of ourselves physically. Sleep, diet, and exercise are a part of that. The health benefits of consistent brisk walking and exercise are many! They improve cardiovascular fitness; strengthen bones and muscles; increase energy levels; improve mood, memory, and sleep; reduce stress and tension; and much more!

If we do not take care of ourselves physically, eventually this will hinder our life and ministry. So, let me encourage you to set aside three to four days each week to spend time taking brisk walks, exercising, and eating healthy meals with those you are on mission with. You won't regret it!

Currently, I run a mile and a half and do one hundred and fifty pushups and crunches three to four times each week when I start my day. I still enjoy good food, but I hold myself accountable by not overeating.

Missional pastors need a weekly Sabbath.

> **Be careful to remember the Sabbath day, to keep it holy as the Lord your God has commanded you. You are to labor six days and do all your work, but the seventh day is a Sabbath to the Lord your God. Do not do any work. (Deuteronomy 5:12–14)**

> For the Lord made the heavens and the earth, the sea, and everything in them in six days; then he rested on the seventh day. Therefore, the Lord blessed the Sabbath day and declared it holy. (Exodus 20:11)

If our Heavenly Father needed a day of rest from his work, you and I need a day of rest from the work he has given us.

Sabbath is defined as "to cease, to stop, or to desist (abstain)." If we understand the work our Heavenly Father has given us and apply ourselves to it weekly, we then need a time of rest each week to cease that work and rest in the Lord. Obviously, that can't be a Sunday, which is a workday for missional pastors—but another day of the week where we don't pile on a to-do list.

My workweek is Sunday to Thursday, with Friday being my day to get all my chores and finances done at home. I observe my weekly Sabbath from 7 p.m. Friday until 7 p.m. Saturday.

I observe the Sabbath as it was meant to be observed, as a day of rest from my work. I usually spend it with my wife and kids.

If we truly observe the Sabbath and make it a day of rest and restoration, that would be fifty-two days a year. That's almost two months of rest, repair, and renewal! Enjoying my Sabbath has brought greater enjoyment out of my vacations. Before I became a Sabbatarian, I would exhaust myself, go on vacation exhausted, and then come back even more exhausted than when I left. Now with a weekly Sabbath, I am getting the rest I need, so when I go on vacation, I can be fully present and enjoy it with my family because I am not exhausted.

Don't abuse your Sabbath. Don't overwork during the week, expecting to catch up on rest and sleep during your Sabbath. If you do, you'll still burn out or be constantly exhausted. A healthy sleep pattern goes hand in hand with a healthy Sabbath.

Again, there are so many benefits to this weekly Sabbath: deeper relationships, reduced stress, increased energy, and support for healthy sleep, to name a few.

We had interns live with us for an extended period of time when we planted a church in East Tennessee. The first week on the mission field, I introduced to them the concept of a weekly Sabbath. After a couple of weeks of missional work, one of my interns told me that he had never needed a Sabbath until he met me! I shared with him that when he found the Lord's work for his life, and he applied himself to it, he would need a Sabbath. We all do.

Missional pastors need like-minded support.

> **Two are better than one because they have a good reward for their efforts. For if either falls, his companion can lift him up; but pity the one who falls without another to lift him up. Also, if two lie down together, they can keep warm; but how can one person alone keep warm? And if someone overpowers one person, two can resist him. A cord of three strands is not easily broken. (Ecclesiastes 4:9–12)**

During an exceptionally stressful season, I met my wife for lunch and shared with her the stresses and weight I currently felt. She looked at me and asked, "Is there someone you can talk with about all this?"

I smiled back at her and said, "Yeah. I am telling you."

Following Jesus isn't for the faint of heart. Preaching the gospel, making disciples, shepherding them well, investing in and redeeming the less fortunate, and developing leaders and teams for the ministry's work can be exhausting at times.

Because of that, we need partners around us who can share in the load of the ministry. If you try to do this alone, you won't go far. Eventually, you will collapse under the weight of the ministry. You will have a moral failure. You will lose your way.

Moses had Aaron. Jesus had the disciples. Paul had Barnabas. Missional pastors need supporting leaders and teams for the work of the ministry.

For many years, I met with a group of pastors where we would encourage one another and spur one another on. We did that every Wednesday at 9 a.m. Each pastor had the opportunity to share their week, highlighting the good, the bad, and the ugly. Then we would pray over him. From time to time, we would really challenge one another if there were things in our lives that shouldn't be there.

To quote a friend, "We should always have a Paul, someone who is pouring into us; we should always have a Barnabas, someone who is the iron who sharpens iron; and a Timothy, someone who we are pouring into. This cord of three strands will not easily be broken."

Supported missional pastors will make an even greater Kingdom Impact.

Reach out to a few leaders you trust and schedule a weekly or biweekly meeting to discuss your lives. Give each other ten to fifteen minutes to share the highs and lows of your week and any areas where you need prayer. Listen to one another. Challenge one another. Pray with one another. This will bless you and them.

Missional pastors need schedules that reflect their priorities and values.

> Commit your activities to the Lord, and your plans will be established. (Proverbs 16:3)

I have always had a mentor. I believe there's something wise about sitting with people who are further down the road in life and ministry.

In 2002–2004, I was mentored by a tremendous pastor from out west. He helped me to write my first Rule of Life and to create a weekly schedule that reflected my values and calling. I've tweaked it over the years, but for the last five-plus years, what I have put on paper here is what was reflected in my schedule every week.

To be clear, if you don't have a Rule of Life or a weekly schedule built around your calling and values, you need to take a couple of days (a couple of days!) and write them out. Then, have your life and support team review them to see if they're realistic.

Below, I give you the "BIG ROCKS" for each day on my calendar. *Big Rocks* are those items of importance that need to be prioritized on your weekly calendar. Big Rocks are the missional pastor's priority.

Sunday Priority: Preaching the gospel (once online, once in person).

Monday Priority: Making disciples in disciple groups (at least two groups: one early, one later).

Tuesday Priority: Shepherding those in my care well (prayer notes to those in my circle of life, coffee and conversations with at least two to three people in my circle of life).

Wednesday Priority: Investing in and redeeming the less fortunate in my community (neighborhood outreach and ministry).

Thursday Priority: Developing leaders and teams for the work of the ministry (one leader coffee, one leader lunch, one team dinner).

Friday Priority: Home to-do list (taking care of the yard, vehicles, finances, etc.).

Saturday Priority: Spending time with my wife and kids on the Sabbath.

This schedule has been tremendously effective for me, and people who know me know my focus on each day.

Does your current schedule reflect your values and calling? Or is it a hodgepodge of a to-do list? I still have to-do lists, but my calling and values are not at the mercy of the urgent.

Missional pastors must have a schedule that reflects their calling and values, or they will not be effective with their God-given time, energy, and resources.

> **So then, each of us will give an account of himself to God. (Romans 14:12)**

www.ingramcontent.com/pod-product-compliance
Lightning Source LLC
Chambersburg PA
CBHW060412050426
42449CB00009B/1958